MEETING · HOME · ECONOMICS

TEXTILES

JAN · COLES

Blackwell Education

Acknowledgments

Aldus Archive pp. 6 bottom ($\times$ 2), 17 bottom left corner, 55 right ($\times$ 2); Allsport (Bob Martin) p. 15 top left corner; Army Headquarters (London) p. 15 top right corner; Laura Ashley pp. 49, 73; British Nuclear Fuels p. 15 bottom right corner; Camera Press pp. 16, 21 top right corner; Mary Evans pp. 6 top, 11 ($\times$ 2); Dan Fedrowicz pp. 65 left, 68; Rosemary Guion pp. 21 bottom left corner; Habitat p. 46 right; Hilltop Road School p. 37; Hulton pp. 58 top, 70 top left corner; ICI Paints pp. 32 ($\times$ 2), 45 right; Ideal Homes p. 44; Japanese Tourist Board p. 76; Marks and Spencers Ltd p. 14; Mothercare p. 48; NASA p. 15 bottom left corner; Christina Newman pp. 8 bottom, 9, 10, 17 bottom right corner, 20, 25 ($\times$ 2), 30 top, 38 top, 45 left, 46 left, 55 left, 56, 62, 68, 70 top right corner, bottom left and right corners, 77 top; Oxford United Football Club p. 58 bottom; Pictorial Colour Slides p. 43 ($\times$ 2); Science Photo Library p. 8 ($\times$ 2) top, 55 middle; John Shelley Photo Library p. 23 ($\times$ 4); Ronald Sheridan p. 36; Katy Squire pp. 17 top right corner, 44 right; Graham Topping pp. 15 bottom, 30 bottom, 38 bottom, 41, 65 right; Xinhua News Agency p. 21; Katie Yelding p. 17 top left corner.

First published 1990

Published by Basil Blackwell Ltd
108 Cowley Road
Oxford OX4 1JF
England

British Library Cataloguing in Publication Data

Coles, Jan
Meeting home economics – textiles.
1. Textiles
I. Title
677
ISBN 0–631–90283–X

Designed by David Chaundy
Illustrated by Nick Davies and Mike Ing
Cover design by Century Guild

Typeset by Opus, Oxford

Printed in Singapore by
Kim Hup Lee Printing Co Pte Limited

Contents

To Jean, with thanks for her help and inspiration.

UNIT 1

Grin and wear it!

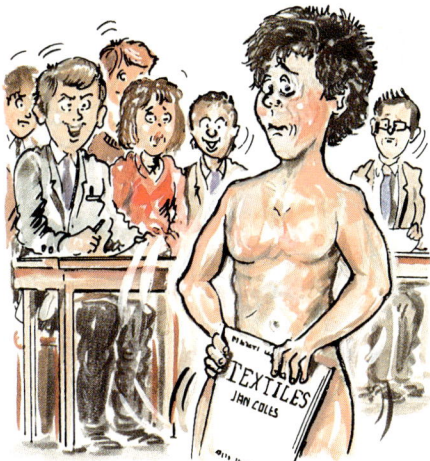

You may be reading this wearing a school uniform or perhaps your own clothes. How would you feel if you had no clothes on at all?! Very red!

Have you ever wondered why you wear clothes? One reason of course is that you'd feel pretty embarrassed sitting there with nothing on!

In this country we are expected to wear clothes most of the time. In fact, it is illegal to be seen naked in most public places. Occasionally, people do go naked as a sort of stunt.

Discuss

1 Can you think of any times when people have got into the newspapers for this?

MOON MADNESS!

Britain's bare bottom bonanza

2 What is it called?
3 What happened to them?

There are some places where it is all right to be naked.

4 When is it all right to be naked?
5 What do you think of the laws about this which we have in this country? Are they too strict?

All change!

In this country we aren't nearly so modest today as we were a century ago.

Observe

Look at this picture of Victorian bathing costumes.

1 What do you think of them?
2 How would you feel wearing something like this?
3 What would these people have thought about the bikini?

Investigate

Find out some of the fashions that have caused a lot of public reaction.

1 For example, what caused a lot of comment in the 1960s? 1970s? 1980s?

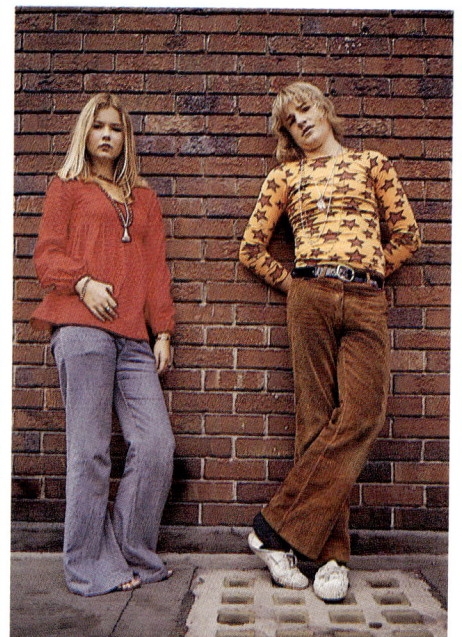

2 Choose one of the fashion extremes.

3 Imagine you are a newspaper reporter at the time when the fashion first became popular.

4 Write your own headlines and report on the new fashion.

Wearing clothes to spare your blushes may be one good reason for doing so. There are many others.

Brainstorm

1 Think of as many reasons as you can for wearing clothes.

2 Make a list of all your ideas.

It may help if you think about the sort of clothes you are wearing now.

- Why are you wearing them?
- Are they the sort of clothes you'd wear at the weekend?
- On holiday?
- In winter or summer?
- To a wedding?
- To play tennis or football?

3 Discuss your list with the rest of the class.

4 Can your ideas be grouped in some way?
For example, we wear clothes for **protection** and **warmth**. What else?

Ranking

1 Try to rank your reasons in order of which are the most important to you.

2 Compare your list with a friend's.

3 Are your reasons in the same order?

4 If not, how do they differ?

Survey

1 Carry out a survey of your parents and grandparents or older brothers and sisters to find out what their most important reasons for wearing clothes are.

2 Present your findings to the rest of the class.

3 Were their reasons different to yours?

4 Whose were? Why might this be so?

Wrap up well!

No doubt one of the reasons you have given for wearing clothes is to keep you warm. How do clothes keep you warm?

What do you do if you are cold? You may well answer 'I put more clothes on!' Well, you are quite right really!

You can keep your body warm by trapping air between layers of fabrics. If you wear several layers of clothing you'll feel warm because air will be trapped between each layer.

Some fabrics are made of fibres which are able to trap air because of certain characteristics that they have. Clothes made of these fabrics will make you feel just as warm as if you were wearing lots of layers of clothing.

Observe

1 Look at the magnified fibres below.

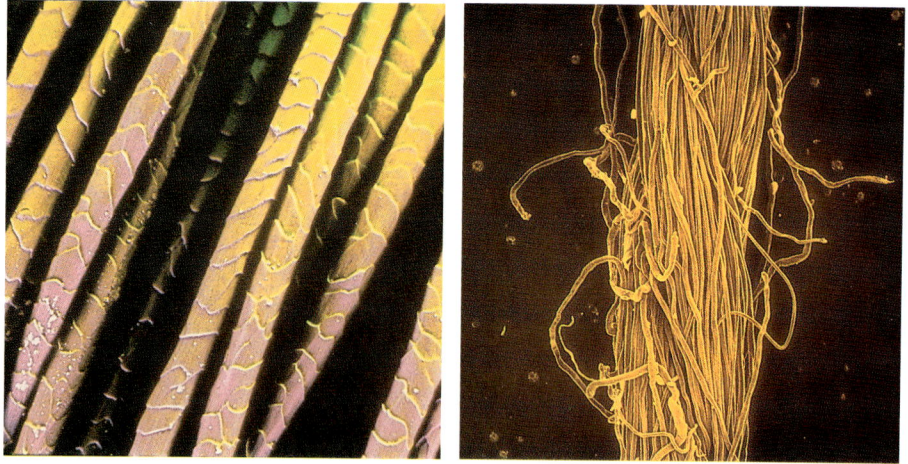

2 Which do you think is more likely to trap air? Why?

Similarly, some yarns are more likely to trap air than others. Can you name some?

3 Now look at these two fabrics.

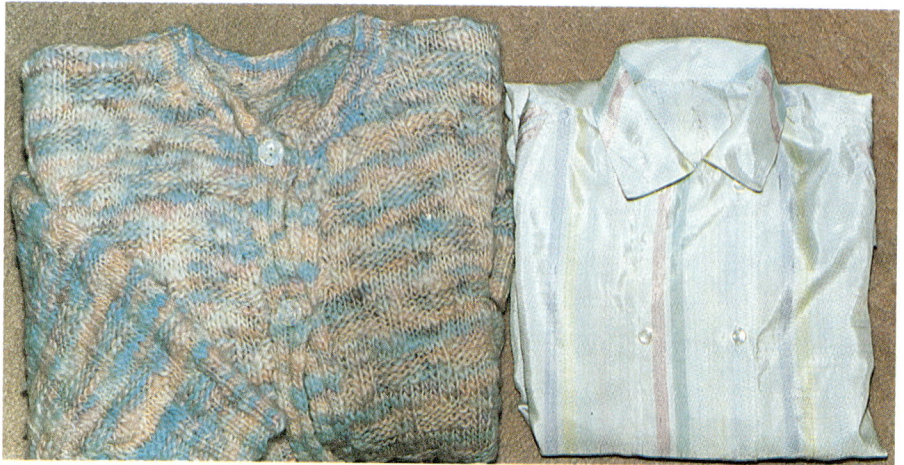

4 Which one would you wear for warmth? Why?

Investigate

1 Find examples or samples of these fabrics.

- A fluffy loose-knit fabric
- A towelling loop pile
- A fleecy dressing gown
- A corduroy fabric
- A smooth cotton
- A fine see-through fabric

2 Rank them in order of which you think would be the warmest to wear.

3 Explain why each fabric is warm or cool.

Investigate

1 Find out the names of some fabrics which we wear because they help us to keep warm. Try to find samples or pictures of your ideas.

Investigate

1 Make a collection of pictures, photographs etc to compare the different types and styles of clothing that you wear for warmth or coolness. You could bring in your own samples!

2 Compare your collection to those of your friends.

Of course the clothes that you wear are just one way of helping to keep your bodies warm. The amount of exercise you do and the foods

you eat will also help you to feel warm. Then there are the different sources of energy you use to heat your homes and workplaces. A layer of trapped air will keep your body warm. This idea can also be used to keep things warm in the home.

How does the idea of trapping air for warmth work in these situations?

a) Keeping food or drink hot?
b) Keeping the heat in a hot-water tank?
c) Linings on curtains?
d) Sleeping with several blankets on your bed in winter?

And so to bed!

Continental quilts have become popular because they can be so warm. Perhaps more important is that they are easy to care for! No more bed-making!

If you sleep under a quilt or duvet you may know what filling it has and what its TOG value is. But do you know why there are different TOG values?

Investigate

Carry out your own investigation into the kinds of quilts or duvets that you can buy.

1 Find out what fillings can be used. What differences do these make?
2 Find out which are more expensive. Why?
3 What does the TOG value mean?
4 Explain how quilts keep you warm.

Stay cool

If keeping warm means trapping air in layers or pockets how would you expect to stay cool?

Brainstorm

1 Imagine you are going on holiday to Spain for a week in the summer.
2 Brainstorm the clothes you would take.
3 Which types of fabrics would your clothes be made of? Why?
4 What other features would you look for in clothes to keep you cool?

EXTENSION WORK

Investigate

1 Make a study of the clothing of people from a different culture to your own.
2 Find out why certain types of clothes are worn. Are there any rules about what clothing people can wear? Unit 11 looks at this in more detail.

Investigate

1 Make a collection of pictures of clothing from another era in history (eg, Victorian, Edwardian).
2 How does the clothing differ from what we wear today?
3 Find out why that style of clothing was worn and what rules or laws there were about clothing in the period you have chosen.

Experiment

We have already discussed the idea that some fabrics are warmer to wear than others. How could you prove this?

1 What experiments could you do to prove that some fabrics keep the heat more than others? Brainstorm your ideas.

2 In pairs or small groups try to plan your own experiment to prove that some fabrics do this. Here are some things you need to think about:

- What fabrics could you use? Why?
- How can you test them to see if they keep the heat?
- What equipment will you need for your experiment?
- How will you make sure your experiment is accurate?
- How will you record your results?
- How will you evaluate your experiment?

This picture might give you some ideas.

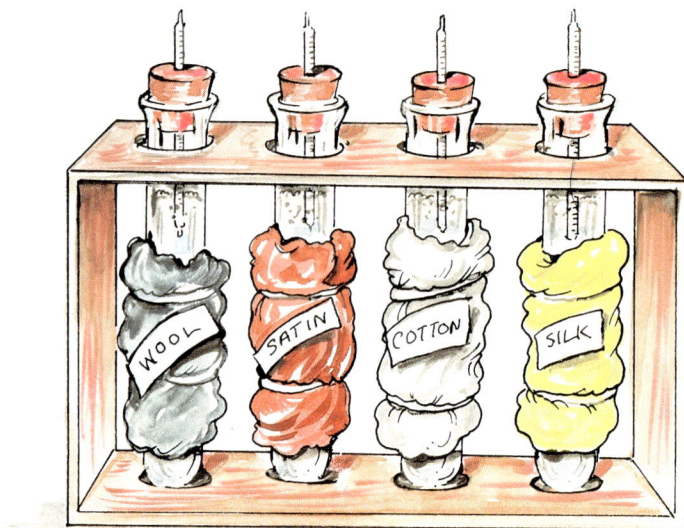

3 When you have planned your experiment see if you can try it out.

Design

Your elderly neighbour suffers from the cold in winter.

1 Design an outfit that she or he could wear to keep warm.
2 Explain what you have chosen to design and how it will keep the person warm.

To help you, here are some practical guidelines.

Guidelines to planning!

1 Sort out what the task is asking you to do. Make a list of the main things you need to think about.
2 Check that your list includes the following items.

- It must keep the person warm
- The person must like it
- It needs to be easy to wear
- It needs to be quite cheap to make

3 Decide how you can find out the information you need to help you do the task.

4 Draw up a plan of action or diary to show how you will go about the task.

Date	Jobs to do	Comments

6 Design your outfit.

7 Explain how it fits the task.

- How does it keep the person warm?
- How much does it cost?
- How does it appeal to older people?

8 Evaluate your work.

- Did you plan the task well?
- Did you do enough research?
- Could you improve any part of your research or planning?
- Was your design suitable?
- How could you find out if it was?

UNIT 2
Knowing who's who

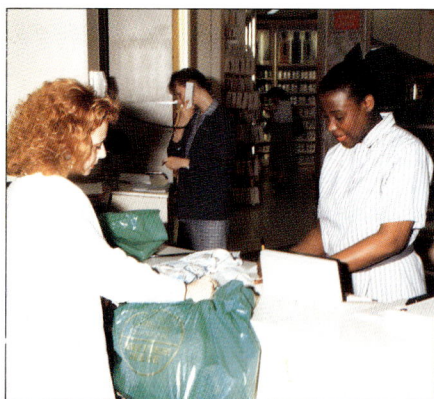

Have you ever been into a shop and asked for help only to find you are asking another customer?

● How do stores help you to know who to ask?

Clothes can be used to identify people. Shop assistants often have a **uniform** so that you know who they are. The uniform may be different for different people working in the shop. Look in a few department stores and note the different uniforms for different staff.

Uniforms can be very helpful in this way. Imagine you were lost at an airport or railway station.

Discuss

1 Who could you ask for help?
2 How would you know who to ask?
3 What if you were injured at a pop concert or a summer fete?

In these cases, spotting someone in uniform who you know can help is very comforting.

4 Think of some other groups of people who wear a uniform which is useful.

Protect yourself

Clothes can be worn or designed to protect you from all kinds of different things. If your job is dangerous or messy, you may need a protective outfit or overall. Maybe you will need special clothes to protect you from the weather. Look at the photos on the next page. Who is wearing a special outfit to prevent him from being seen?

Brainstorm

1 Think of all the different people who wear clothes for protection.
2 What are they being protected from?
3 How do their clothes protect them?

Surgeons wear gowns to prevent patients from being infected in any way. They also wear gowns to protect themselves against infection from the patient's blood, for example.

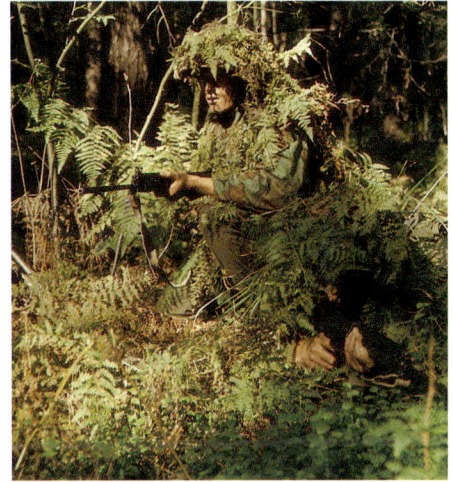

Think of some other groups of people who wear protective clothes for these reasons.

Bright is right!

There are other ways of protecting yourself using different items of clothing or fabrics. Cyclists wear fluorescent strips of fabric which show up in the dark to let other road users know they are there.

● Which other people wear bright clothes to help them to be seen?

Discuss

Many schools have a uniform of some kind.

1 Why do you think this is?
2 Do you agree that schools should have a uniform?
3 What reasons can you think of for and against having a uniform?

'But everybody looks the same!'

A lot of people do not like school uniform. This is probably because they want to be different. They don't like looking the same as everyone else. Why is this?

Sometimes the clothes we wear to be fashionable are a kind of uniform.

- What do you wear at the week-ends?
- Would you wear the same as your friend?
- How many of you in your class or group have similar sorts of clothes?

Brainstorm

1 Can you think of any groups of people who wear a 'fashion' uniform?
2 Ask an older person if they knew of any groups like this when they were younger.

Even football and rugby teams have a uniform – as do most sports.

Brainstorm

1 List all the games, sports and other special activities you take part in.
2 List the clothing you wear for each.
3 What type of protection is needed for each sport or activity?
4 How are you protected?

In these cases the 'uniform' means you are part of a group or team. It makes you feel that you 'belong'. This is an important feeling.

Design

1 Design a jogging suit or tee-shirt with a logo for a local sports team of your choice who have got through to national finals.
   a) What do you need to discuss with the team before you start your design?

b) What designs would you suggest?

c) Give reasons for your choice of design.

First impressions

Why do people want to be different? It's all to do with what you want to tell other people about yourself. That is the **image** you want to put over. If you are wearing school uniform right now there isn't much that people can learn about you as a person.

- What kind of image would you be giving people if you were wearing your own clothes?

Observe

1 Look at the pictures below.

2 What sort of person do you think each of these people is? How would you describe them?

3 Pick one or two labels from the list below, to describe each person.

Add your own labels to the list.

- Poser
- Expensive
- Smart
- Pretty
- Attention seeking
- Casual
- Rebellious
- Individual
- Dirty
- Severe
- Feminine
- Demure
- Trendy
- Fun
- Business-like

- Fashionable
- Impressive
- Handsome
- Shocking
- Tom boy
- Friendly
- Part of a group or cult
- Scruffy
- Cuddly
- Sophisticated
- Dull
- Fit
- Masculine
- Plain
- Efficient

4 Discuss your labels with others in your group.
5 Do you all agree on the labels?
6 Was it their clothes that helped you to decide what label to give them?

Clothes tell you a lot about a person.

- Which image labels apply to you?

Observe

1 Bring your favourite set of clothes into your next lesson.
2 Ask your friends to give you an image label.
3 How did they decide on that label?
4 Is it the kind of label you want to have?

The image you give people by your clothes depends on two things.

- What the people looking at you actually see.
- How they interpret what they see.

This is why the image you think you are giving may differ from the one others see. What a thought!

What an occasion . . . ?

Often we dress differently for different occasions or situations.

Brainstorm

1 Think of occasions when you might dress differently from usual.

Sometimes people dress in a certain way deliberately. They want to create a certain image.

Margaret Thatcher is often described as having a 'soft' look or an 'I mean business' look. The image she wishes to give people depends on the situation she is in.

- Have you ever dressed to create a certain image?

Discuss

1 What would you wear for each of these situations?
    a) An interview at college or for a job
    b) Meeting your girl or boyfriend's parents
    c) A disco
    d) Your first date with a new girl or boyfriend
    e) A driving test

2 Do you think it should matter what you wear? Why? Why not?

I'll wear what I like!

Be honest – how often have you worn something because you knew it might shock people? Or to rebel against someone?

Describe, draw or show a photo of yourself.

Clothes often cause arguments between parents and teenagers.

Discuss

1 Have you ever been in this kind of situation?
2 What usually happens?
3 What are the parents complaining about?
4 Do you think your parents were ever in trouble for this?
5 What kind of clothes might they have worn?

What is the answer to this kind of problem?

Design

1 Design a new outfit to shock your parents and/or teachers.
2 Explain why you feel it would shock people?
3 Would you wear it?

Where does your image come from?

One of the biggest influences on the image you want is the **media**.

Discuss

What kinds of images of teenagers are shown on television? In magazines?

1 Do you ever find yourself wanting to be like them?
2 Do you ever feel they are too perfect in any way?

The images we get from television and other forms of the media are looked at more in Unit 5 in the Home Section of *Home and Family*.

Investigate

1 Make a study of your favourite selection of magazines or television programmes for teenagers.
2 In groups discuss:
   a) The image of youth in the magazines or programmes. Is it real? How? How not?
   b) Have you ever been in any of the situations described in the stories?
   c) Are the images for boys and girls different in the magazines or programmes? How?
      • What are the boys like?
      • What are the girls like?
3 Write a story or scene to go into one of the magazines or television programmes.

EXTENSION WORK Design

Some of your friends have set up a pop group to play at your local disco. They want advice on what to wear. They want to have a certain image.

1 What would you talk to them about?
2 Decide on an image for them
3 How would you go about designing the image that they want?
4 Present your ideas for designs that they could use.

Design

You have been asked to give advice on a uniform for teenagers working in a new fast-food restaurant that is opening in your area.

1 Design a uniform suitable for teenage helpers who will be employed as waiters and waitresses in the restaurant.
2 Give reasons for your choice of design.

Observe

People in different countries wear different clothes for certain occasions.

1 Look at the pictures below.

2 For each picture try to identify
   a) The country
   b) The occasion

UNIT 3
It's the fashion

When was the last time you bought some clothes or a new outfit? What did you buy? Can you say why you bought these clothes?

Talk through your ideas with a friend.

Have a look at this list of reasons:

- Everyone has got them
- It was all I could afford
- I felt like buying something bright
- I saw it in a magazine
- I saw it in the window
- It's the fashion
- I was fed-up
- I was going to a party

Discuss

1 Have you ever bought clothes for any of these reasons?
2 Which ones?
3 Can you add anything else to this list?

It may be that you needed cheering up or that you just saw something and wanted it. Maybe you had a special occasion to go to and wanted something new to wear. These are all reasons why we buy new clothes. If you follow fashion then you will probably buy clothes to keep up with new trends. Keeping up with the fashion is very important for some people. It is a part of their image. They are looked upon as 'go ahead' and 'up to date'.

The fashion setters

Two of the most popular fashion setters at the moment are the Princess of Wales and the Duchess of York (Fergie).

Investigate

1 Make a collection of photos or articles about the clothes worn by the Princess of Wales and the Duchess of York over the past few years.
2 What fashion trends have they started?
3 Have you adopted any of these styles? Which ones?

4 What about other people in your class? Which styles do they like?

Princess Diana and Fergie are very much in the public eye. All over the world people look to them as fashion setters. Their clothes get a lot of publicity. Sometimes they are criticised for wearing the 'wrong' thing or for wearing something which does not suit them.

What comments would you make about the clothes they wear?

Forever changing

Fashion never stands still. New designs are always being created. Old designs are sometimes brought back into fashion.

Discuss

1 What are the fashion trends at the moment?
2 Are there any styles which have been around before?
3 What were the trends last year?
4 What do you think will be the trend next year?

Investigate

1 Choose an aspect or item of clothing.
2 Trace the fashion changes that have taken place in that one aspect over the last ten or twenty years.
3 Present your study to the rest of your class.
4 Which items of clothing have changed most over the years?
5 Why is this?

Sometimes fashion makes us wear things which aren't fit for the purpose or occasion. Some people would rather look really fashionable than be sensible or comfortable. That's the power of fashion!

Observe

Look at these pictures.

1 Why isn't the choice of clothing very sensible?
2 Have you ever been in these kinds of situations? When? What were you wearing?

I feel great!

You may have found in your investigations that a lot of people wear the clothes that they feel most comfortable in. There are some clothes which simply feel right. They may not be the height of fashion but they are what people like to wear.

Some people don't feel right without a tie on. Others feel uncomfortable when they wear one. Some women like to wear trousers. Others don't.

Discuss

1 What kind of clothes do you feel most comfortable in?
2 Describe them or bring them into school if you can.
3 Is everyone's choice different?

Survey

1 Ask different people about the kinds of clothes they wear for comfort.
2 Find out why they feel comfortable in these clothes.
3 Record their answers.
4 Report back to the rest of your class.
5 Can you draw any conclusions from your survey? What makes clothes comfortable?

Seven different me's!

Did you know that the mood you're in and the way you feel can affect your choice of clothes?

Your wardrobe probably has a range of different clothes in it. What you choose to wear will depend on the way you are feeling.

Sometimes if you're fed-up you treat yourself to some new clothes. They may be bright to cheer you up, or sombre because that is how you felt at the time.

In just the same way, if you are feeling happy you may pick certain clothes to wear. You may not realise you are doing this, but you are. It's in your subconscious!

Brainstorm

1 What clothes would you wear if you felt in these moods?

- Quiet
- Devilish
- Get up and go
- Notice me
- Don't notice me
- Fed-up
- Party mood

Did you describe colours of clothes to suit these moods? No doubt you did. Colour plays a very important part in our lives as you will see in Unit 4.

For now though, take a look around you next time you are in town. Notice what people are wearing.

- What do their clothes tell you?
- What kind of person are you looking at?
- What kind of mood are they in?

EXTENSION WORK   *Design*

Design an outfit for a teenager to wear to a disco in the winter. The disco will be hot but it will be cold outside.

Draw up a plan of action (see the **EXTENSION WORK** in Unit 1). Use the following list of questions to help you.

1 What have you been asked to do?
2 Make a list of the things you need to think about before you can design the outfit.
3 Where will you get the information from to help you?
4 Draw up a plan of action to show what you'll do and when.
5 Carry out your plan of action.
6 Draw your designs.
7 Give reasons for your choices of designs.
8 Evaluate your work. What questions will you ask?

Investigate

1 Find out the names of some present-day fashion designers.
2 What styles have they introduced?
3 Which of these styles do you or would you wear?
4 Do they design for any famous people?
   • Collect pictures/articles of their designs.

UNIT 4

A splash of colour

Colour is a normal everyday part of our world. It is something that we often take for granted.

- What would the world be like without colour?

Very few of us would choose a black and white television or black and white photos.

Why is this?

Brainstorm

1 What is so important about colour?
2 If there were no colours, would this be a disadvantage?
3 What would be the problems in a black and white world?
4 Brainstorm your ideas as a group.

Feeling blue

Colours are often linked to moods, feelings and situations.

For example:

- Green with envy
- Feeling blue
- Purple with rage
- White as a sheet
- A black mood

Discuss

1 Can you think of any other examples?
2 Can you explain them to the rest of the class?

We wear different coloured clothes to suit the mood we are in. (See Unit 3.)

People react to colours in several different ways. How do you feel about different colours?

Discuss

1 Do you have a favourite colour?
2 Why do you like it?
3 What colours do you hate?
4 Which colours make you feel cheerful? Warm? Relaxed?
5 Why do they make you feel like this?

Survey

1 Find out what answers the people in your class have given to these questions. Are they all different?
2 Try asking older people, too.
3 What conclusions can you draw about people's reactions to colours?

Survey

1 From a range of people of your age, find out which colours are
   a) Most popular at the moment
   b) Least popular at the moment

Investigate

1 Find out which colours are most popular with young children.
2 Look at some of the toys for young children that are sold in the shops. Which colours are used?
3 Why do you think these colours are used?

Colour constancy

We rely on colour constancy. This means that we expect things to stay the same 'normal' colour. This helps us to make sense of the world. For example, grass is green. We would think there was something very wrong if it looked blue or red. We also rely on colour to help us make decisions. For example, the colour of food is very important to us.

1 Would you eat green mashed potato?
2 Black baked beans?
3 Blue sausages?

Food manufacturers add colour to some foods to make them more appealing to us. For example, fish fingers are coated in orange

breadcrumbs. But have you ever seen orange bread or bread-crumbs before?

We get so used to the colours added to foods by manufacturers that we think the natural colours are dull and insipid.

Brainstorm

1 Do you know of any other foods which have colour added? Which ones?

Children especially, like brightly coloured foods.

2 Think of some of the brightly coloured foods that children like to eat.

Where do colours come from?

They come from white light! Different waves (**frequencies**) of light are seen as different colours. Our eyes receive these light waves, in just the same way as our ears pick up sound waves.

- When do you see white light being split up into different colours?
- What are the colours?

Most objects absorb or reflect certain frequencies of light waves. The combination of the reflected frequencies results in the colour that we see.

For example, green grass is reflecting green light rays.

- What colour light rays are reflected by the clothes you are wearing now?

I can't tell what colour this is . . .

Colours look different in different lights. At night, everything looks dark. In the light, some substances absorb parts of the visible light. In the daylight, colours can look different to when they are in artificial lighting.

- Have you ever bought something from a shop only to find it looked a different colour when you got outside?
- Have you ever noticed how the colour of your clothes changes in disco lights?

Mix 'n' match

Colour can be divided into three main types. These are

1 **Primary** colours
2 **Secondary** colours
3 **Tertiary** colours

The links between these three types of colour can be seen by studying the colour wheel below.

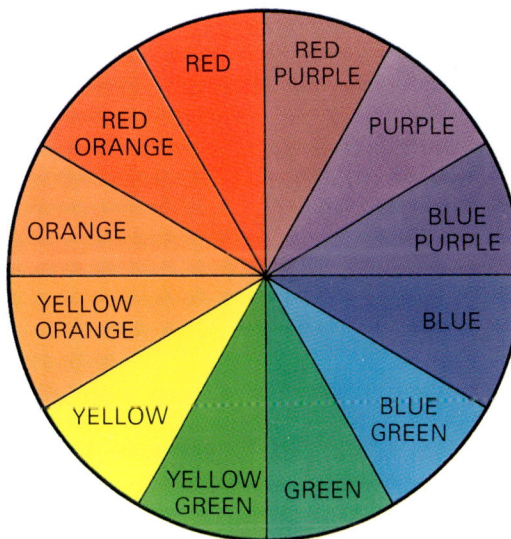

The primary colours are **red**, **yellow** and **blue**. Primary means that they cannot be mixed from other colours.

The secondary colours are **orange**, **green** and **purple**. These can be mixed from two primary colours.

The tertiary colours are mixed from the colours which are next to one another on the colour wheel.

What about brown? This colour is different. Brown is made by mixing all three primary colours.

- Try this out!

Colours for warmth

Colours are often talked about as being 'warm' or 'cool'.

Investigation

1 Carry out a survey of your family or friends to find out:
  a) Which colours they think of as being warm
  b) Which colours they think of as being cool

2 Are there any colours which could be both warm and cool? Which ones?
3 What colours would you choose for a bedroom facing north?
4 What would you choose for a south-facing kitchen?

Colour schemes

There are lots of words we can use to describe colours. You have probably come across quite a few new words already!

● The scientific name of a colour is a **hue**.

So, red, orange, yellow, green, blue and purple are all hues.

A hue may be light or dark. For example, we have light blue and dark blue.

● A **tint** is any colour with white added to it.
● A **shade** is any colour with black added to it.

So, light blue is a tint and dark blue is a shade.

● What is dark red?
● What is light green?

Investigate

1 Pick a hue.
2 Find or list as many tints as you can for the hue you have chosen.

3 Find or list as many shades as you can for the hue you have chosen.

4 Report your findings to the rest of your class.

Colours that are opposite to one another on the colour wheel are called **complements**. In other words, they are in contrast to one another.

Colours next to one another on the colour wheel are **harmonies**. In other words, they are similar because they have a hue in common.

Observe

Look at the colour wheel.

1 Name two colours which are complements.

2 Name two colours which are harmonies.

Investigate

1 Choose a hue.

2 Produce an example of a colour scheme for an outfit which uses complementary colours.

3 Produce an example of a colour scheme using harmonious colours.

4 Show your scheme to the rest of your class.

Colour my world

Colour can have an amazing effect on the world we live in. It can make us feel happy or sad, angry or calm. It can please us or horrify us. It can make objects seem bigger or smaller. It can make objects seem nearer or at a distance.

How does it do this?

Experiment

1 Plan your own experiment to show how different colours can make rooms look
  a) Larger
  b) Smaller

2 Explain your experiment to the rest of your class.

Investigate

A friend of yours is trying to slim.

1 Which colours would you advise your friend to wear?

2 Which colours should your friend avoid wearing?

Patterns can also have a similar effect. Large bold patterns on a wall can make the room seem small. Small patterns can be lost in a large room.

Experiment

1 Carry out an experiment with different patterns on clothing to show how they can affect
   a) Tall people
   b) Small people

Whatever you feel about colour you have to think about several things when you are choosing colours for clothes or for the home.

Your choice of colours depends on what you like, how you feel and, of course, what is in fashion.

Colours go in and out of fashion just as styles of clothes do.

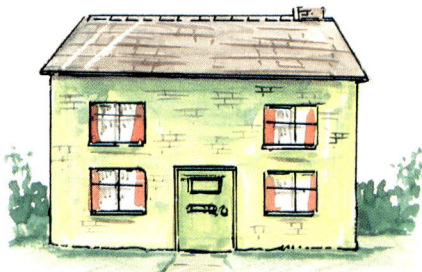

Discuss

1 Which colours are in fashion for the home at the moment?
2 How would you feel about each of these?

- A red kitchen
- A black classroom
- A lime green house
- An orange bedroom
- A purple bathroom
- A grey hospital ward

Research

1 Collect some pictures of rooms using different colour schemes. They may be schemes which you like or dislike.
2 What do you think of each one?
3 Which ones do you like best? Why?
4 What effect do the colours have on each of the rooms?

Brainstorm

You have been asked to choose a colour scheme for the living room in a new house.

1 What must you think about before deciding on a colour scheme?

EXTENSION WORK ### Investigate

You have been asked to plan the colour schemes for a new house.

1 What colours would you choose for each of these rooms in the house:
   a) A large, north-facing living room
   b) A small, sunny kitchen
   c) A small, dark bathroom with no window
   d) A large bedroom with a high ceiling

Investigate

Colours often have symbolic meanings. People wear different colours for different festivals and occasions.

1 Find out what colours are worn in different countries of your choice for:
   a) Weddings
   b) Funerals
2 Find out which colours are worn by Bhuddist monks, nuns, rabbis, and officials of the Sikh and Hindu faiths.
3 Why do they wear different colours?

UNIT 5
Let's get creative!

Many textiles, and especially clothes, are decorative. But to an artist textiles can also be used to express ideas and thoughts.

Tapestry

Tapestries were originally made to decorate the walls of castles, monasteries and great houses. Tapestries are made out of fabrics and yarns stiched into a background cloth. The most famous tapestry is the **Bayeux tapestry**. It was made in the eleventh century and shows scenes from the Battle of Hastings.

Investigate

1 Look at the photograph showing part of the Bayeux tapestry.
2 What scenes is it showing?
3 Describe the story it is illustrating.

Design

1 Think about a usual day in your life.
2 Draw a design for a tapestry which will illustrate your day.

Collage

Textiles, yarns and scraps of fabric can be used to build up a picture (a **collage**) which may have a three-dimensional effect. All sorts of different fabrics can be used and when they are glued or stiched onto a background, they give a very interesting and unusual effect. A picture of a cat can now be given a furry coat!

Design

1 Collect a selection of fabric pieces, yarns and other textiles from around your home. (Your teacher will probably have a lot of material you can use.)
2 Using glue and sewing stitches, make a collage from your materials.

You can also use card, wood, metal, stone, feathers, grass and buttons to create your picture.

Embroidery

Thread and very small pieces of fabric can be used to embroider pictures. At one time young girls being brought up in richer families made samplers by embroidery. These were small pictures or quotes from the Bible. Being able to embroider beautiful samplers and sew well was seen to be a very important part of a young woman's education.

There are many other crafts which use textiles. Oil painters use canvas tacked on to a wooden frame to paint on.

Investigate

Investigate

1 Find out about one of the following:
   a Appliqué
   b Lace making
   c Macramé
2 How are textiles used in each of these crafts?
3 Collect samples or pictures which show these activities and their products.

Clothes can be decorated using some of the techniques mentioned above. For example, garments can be embroidered to give an unusual and unique decoration. Have any of your clothes been embroidered? Designs can also be put onto a piece of clothing by appliqué. A pattern is built up by sewing pieces of other fabric onto the garment to make a picture. The picture could be an abstract design or of a specific object – maybe a person or an animal.

What other techniques can you think of that we use to decorate materials with?

Dyeing and printing

As we saw in Unit 4, colour is a very important part of our world and of the textiles that we use. How are different fabrics given their different colours. Obviously, wool doesn't have a wide range of colour naturally. Have you ever seen a sheep with red or blue fleece?

"I'll have a green pair of socks, a blue jumper,…"

So how do fabrics get their colours?

Hundreds of years ago, peasants wore dull and drab clothes because these were the natural colours of the skins and wool they used. Only the rich people could afford to dye their clothes. Ancient Britons used **woad**, a blue dye, to decorate themselves and their clothes. Other natural dyes which were used were saffron, an orange-yellow dye which came from the autumn crocus, and royal purple, from a species of Mediterranean whelk.

Nowadays, most dyes are made from chemicals. Dyes can either be added to the fibres themselves, or to the yarn, or to the fabric before or after it has been made into a garment. Dyes must be chosen carefully. Different dyes work better on some fabrics than on others. Also, the dye must be **fast**. This means that the colour doesn't fade in sunlight or **run** when it comes into contact with water.

Tie-dyeing is one method of adding colour to a fabric and creates unusual and interesting designs. Tie-dyeing can be done either before or after a fabric has been made into a garment.

The fabric is folded, knotted, tied or sewn in such a way that when the fabric is immersed in the dye, colour does not get into some areas. Other special effects can be produced by tying marbles or buttons into the fabric.

Investigate

1 Wash, rinse and dry the piece of fabric or garment you wish to dye.
2 Make up a solution of shop-bought, cold-water dye according to the instructions on the packet.

3 Tie up the fabric as shown in the picture.
4 Wet the fabric and leave in the dye solution for 30 minutes to 1 hour. Stir for the first 10 minutes.
5 Remove the fabric carefully. Wash and rinse the sample in hot water.
6 Iron the fabric dry.

What kinds of pattern have you produced? Repeat the process using different methods of tying the fabric and compare the patterns that you produce.

When a fabric is dyed both sides of the fabric are coloured. **Printing** colours only one side of the fabric and can be used to produce a very complicated and intricate pattern.

The easiest way to print is to cut the pattern you want out of a block. Dye is then applied to this surface and the block is then laid on the fabric.

● You will probably have tried block printing at school, using a pattern cut out of a potato.

Block printing is very slow, so in industry, the process is speeded up by cutting the pattern on a roller. The material being printed can then be passed around the roller in a long, continuous strip.

This type of printing, called roller printing, does not produce a very sharp pattern. To get greater detail, screen printing is used. This type of printing is very similar to stenciling. The design you want on the fabric is cut out of film and laid out on a screen of silk or nylon. Dye can only pass through certain areas. The pattern cut out of the film is transferred onto the fabric.

Another industrial printing technique is transfer printing.

Investigate

1 Use resources (either at home or at school) to find out about transfer printing.
2 What sort of fabrics does this technique work best with?
3 What are the drawbacks of transfer printing?

2 Discuss your ideas with a friend.

It might help to think about the answers to the following questions.

- Did you choose certain soft furnishings because you needed them?
- What would a room be like without curtains or lampshades?
- Did you choose anything because it added 'atmosphere' or matched a particular theme you had?

3 Compare your room design with that of a friend. Are your designs similar? Different? In what ways?

It goes with my image!

In Unit 2 we looked at how we choose clothes to fit in with our image. You may have given yourself an image label if you worked through the unit. In other words you may have decided that you dress in a particular way in order to look sophisticated or outrageous or tough . . . ?

Discuss

1 What image label would you give to your room?

- cool
- feminine
- bright
- calm
- sophisticated
- soft
- masculine
- peaceful
- heavy

2 Has your room got a similar image to you?

You've made your bed . . . now lie in it!

You may have found that your personal image is different to the one that your room has. Why is this? Perhaps this cartoon will give you a clue . . .

When you choose furniture and soft furnishings for a room they have to be choices that you can live with for quite some time. It would be very expensive to change the style of your room as often as you might change the style of your clothes!

This may be why the image of your room is different to the one you reflect through the clothes you wear.

Investigate

1 Work in groups. Collect as many different images for each of these rooms in a house as you can.
   a) Bedrooms
   b) Kitchens
   c) Bathrooms

Looks nice

Keeps noise in or out

Keeps light out

For warmth

Cuts down on draughts

A good fit

For comfort

2 Give each one an image label.
3 Explain your labels to a friend.

The case of the missing budgie!

What's this got to do with budgies? Well, whether you are an ardent budgie lover or not you will know that budgies are often kept in cages and that at night they like the cage to be covered over.

Why do you think this is? Look at this picture.

The budgie cage cover has many uses. It keeps out the noise. It keeps out the light. It may even help to keep the budgie a bit warmer.

This example shows how many different reasons there are for choosing soft furnishings... and the story does not end here...

I can't afford it!

How often do you say this to yourself or have had it said to you?

You can't always use the reason that you like something as an excuse for having it. If you haven't got enough money then you may need to think again or save up like mad!

There are also other things which can become priorities when you are choosing what to put in your room. These will depend upon your family situation and your circumstances.

For example, if there are toddlers around the house, you may choose different soft furnishings than if you were living on your own.

Discuss

1 What would you need to think about if you were choosing soft furnishings for a toddler's room?
2 Discuss your ideas with a friend.

Investigate

Many old people feel the cold badly. Sometimes they live in old, draughty houses.

1 Find out the main areas where heat is lost in the home.
2 How can soft furnishings be used to help them to keep their homes warm?
3 Suggest ways that old people can insulate their homes, fairly cheaply.

Design

1 Plan the soft furnishings that you would choose for a baby's bedroom.

2 Give details of what you would choose and why.

3 Include a plan of the room as part of your study.

In general, you will find that your choice of soft furnishings will depend upon the following factors:

- Who they are for
- How much you have to spend
- What the house is like
- What the person feels happy with

There are many points to think about before you decide upon the furnishings for a home.

There are also many things you can learn about people from the soft furnishings that they choose! Next time you pay someone a visit have a look at their choice of furnishings. What kind of people do you think they are? What kind of image do they put across?

EXTENSION WORK *Investigate*

There are many types of carpeting available today.

1 Find out about the range of carpets you can buy.

2 Compare the costs of the different ranges.

3 Suggest a type of carpet for each of these rooms. Give reasons for your choices.
   a) Bedroom   **b)** Stairway   **c)** Kitchen

Investigate

1 Make a collection of samples of each of the items below
   a) Furnishing fabrics   **c)** Carpets
   b) Wallpapers

2 Explain how different textures and patterns can affect the look of a room.

Investigate

1 Find out the names of some present-day designers of soft furnishings. An example might be a Laura Ashley collection.
2 What sort of image do the designs have?

Design

1 Design an item of soft furnishing for yourself or your family.
2 Give reasons for your choice of item.

Don't forget to make a plan of action!

UNIT 7
A world of fabrics

What do we use fabrics for?

The chances are that you would answer 'for clothes'.
Did most people in your class give this answer? Carry out a quick survey.

Most people think of clothing when they are asked this question. And of course, they are quite right! If you have worked through Unit 6, you will also know of some uses of fabrics in the home.

Can you give some examples?

However, fabrics and fibres are used for many more things than you'd think of at first.

Look at the picture below.

Observe

1 List all the different items in the picture which are made of some kind of fabric.
2 Can you think of any more items that could be added to the picture?
3 Share your list with a friend.

- How many items have you got altogether?
- Are you surprised by the amount?

Beaches aren't the only places where you can find lots of examples of different fabrics. Fabrics are used everywhere. Have you ever thought of all the different fabrics used in hospitals? In sport? In accidents and emergencies? On a camping holiday? In industry? How does an artist make use of different fabrics?

Brainstorm

1 Brainstorm as many different situations as you can that make use of fabrics.

Design

1 Draw your own scene or situation to show as many different uses of fabrics as you can.
2 Ask a friend to spot all the different uses.
3 How many did she or he get?

The right fabric for the job

Do you think is matters which fabrics are used for each of the items in your picture?

The answer to that question is quite simply 'Yes'!
Many different fabrics will have been used in making the wide variety of items.

Brainstorm

1 Why are different types of fabrics used to make different items?
2 Brainstorm your ideas with some friends.

Perhaps this example will help you to explain . . .

1 A deckchair is made from a fabric which is

- Strong
- Firm
- Hard-wearing
- Comfortable
- Fairly weather-resistant

Discuss

1 What would happen if it wasn't any of these?

2 Describe or draw a picture of what might happen if the deckchair was made of a J-cloth type material!

3 Why would you dry yourself with a towel, and not with a groundsheet-type fabric after you have been swimming?

You have been thinking about the **properties** of the different fabrics used. Each fabric has certain properties which make it right for the job it has to do.

Discuss

1 What is meant by the word properties? Discuss your ideas as a group.
2 Try to come up with a definition of the word.

Discuss

1 Look back at your list of items made from fabric.
2 Choose six very different items.
3 What fabrics are the items made from?
4 What are the properties of the fabrics which make them right for the jobs they are doing?

Item	Properties of the fabric it is made from	Why these properties are important
Towel	absorbent (mops up water)	so that it dries properly
	strong	so it can be washed a lot, and can be wrapped and pulled round you
	soft	so it is gentle on your skin

5 Why are these properties important? Make a table like this one.
6 Discuss your ideas with a friend.

A closer look at properties

So far you have been thinking about the different properties of fabrics which make them right for the jobs they have to do. There is a very large number of different properties for the different fabrics that are used. There are even more than you listed above.

Brainstorm

1 Brainstorm as many different fabric properties as you can. Use other text books or computer data files to help you.
2 Make a collection of as many different fabrics as you can.
3 Try to describe the properties that each of the fabrics have. Use the list you made in part **1** and the following words to help you.

- Soft
- Hard-wearing
- Stretchy
- Water-proof
- Cool
- Warm
- Absorbent

- Light-weight
- Heavy-weight
- Strong
- Smooth
- Open texture
- Close-knit texture
- Rough

4 Discuss your ideas with a friend.
5 What do you think each fabric could be used for? Make a list of your ideas.
6 Report your findings to the others in your class.

All the properties that you have looked at and talked about are important. Each of them can be used in certain situations to do certain jobs. Can you work out the importance of some of these properties for yourself?

Investigate

1 Choose three or four of the properties you thought of in the last brainstorming exercise.
2 For each property, decide
  a) Why that property is important.
  b) When the property is useful.

Here is an example to help you.

Property	Why it is important	When it is useful
Absorbency	It means it will dry things properly	Towels, nappies, mops, sportswear

How could you test fabrics to see if they have some of these properties? What would you have to do?

Try this experiment to test the flammability of different fabrics.

Experiment

Use fabric samples of wool, cotton and polyester.

1 Cut 30 cm × 5 cm lengths of each fabric.
2 Peg the end of each strip to a wire line suspended off the ground.

- Only do the experiment with one piece of fabric at a time.

3 Set each strip alight and watch what happens?
  a) How quickly does the fabric ignite?
  b) How long does it take for the whole strip to burn?
  c) What does it smell like when it is burning?

Experiment

1 Plan experiments to test a range of fabrics for some of these properties.
  a) Strength
  b) Warmth
  c) Absorbency
  d) Comfortable to touch
2 Carry out your experiment.
3 Present your results to the rest of your group.

- Do any fabrics have all of the properties you chose?
- Do any have only one?
- What conclusions can you draw from your results?

Why use fabrics at all?

Have you ever wondered why fabric is used to make so many different things?

Discuss

1 Look back at the picture of the beach scene on page 50.
2 Imagine the items in the picture are made of
  a) Plastic
  b) Paper
  c) Cardboard
  d) Foil
3 What would they be like?
4 Which of the items could be made of paper or plastic?
5 Which of them could not? Why not?
6 Which ones could be made of foil or cardboard?

The problem with using any of these materials is that they are not very **versatile**. In other words, they don't have as many different properties as fabrics do.

- Paper isn't strong enough to use as deckchair material.

- A cardboard wind break is not waterproof.
- A plastic bathing costume would feel pretty uncomfortable.
- What is wrong with using a plastic towel?

BUT! Marathon runners are given a foil blanket when they finish a race. Why?

Brainstorm

1 Think of some other advantages and disadvantages of using paper, foil or plastic instead of fabrics.

Fabrics may be 'born' with certain properties. This depends on where or what they came from.

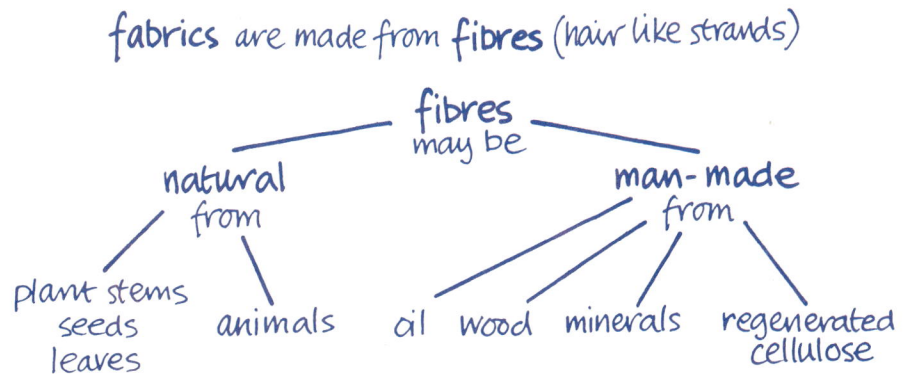

fabrics are made from **fibres** (hair like strands)

fibres may be

natural from — plant stems, seeds, leaves — animals

man-made from — oil, wood, minerals, regenerated cellulose

- Can you name some fabrics which are
  a) From natural sources?
  b) Man-made?

The sources shown below are all natural sources.

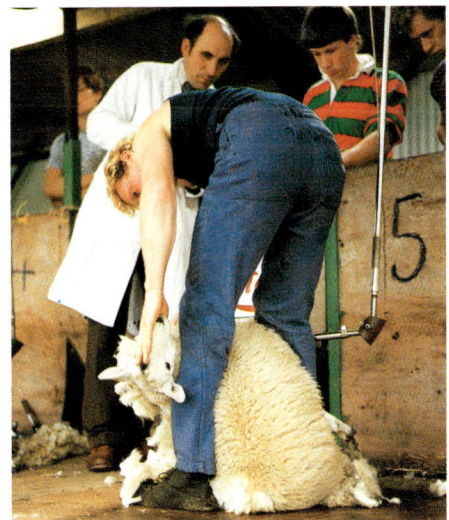

Investigate

1 Find out how silk is produced.
2 Can you explain why it is so expensive?

Observe

1 Collect as many different fibres as you can from both natural and man-made fabrics.
2 Use a microscope to see what they look like.
3 Find out the properties of these fibres.

Spinning a yarn . . .

Fibres are usually made into yarns. This is done by spinning (twisting) the fibres together. The way that the fibres are spun will affect the properties of the final fabric. For example, yarns can be made thicker or thinner by spinning more or less fibres together. They can be made to feel hard or soft by changing the amount of twist. Loose twisting of fibres gives a softer yarn. Tight twisting gives a firm thread.

Yarns are made into fabrics. This may be done by knitting or weaving the yarn. A knitted yarn will have many different properties to one that has been woven. The way that the yarns are knitted or woven will also give different properties to the final fabric.

Investigate

1 Find out about as many different types of yarn as you can.
2 How do these yarns affect the properties of a fabric?

Investigate

1 Find out more about how cotton yarn is made.
2 Explain your findings to the rest of the class.

Sometimes, manufacturers make use of the properties of two fibres when making a fabric. In other words, fibres may be blended or yarns may be mixed.

Today, cotton is blended with other fibres such as wool, nylon, polyester and rayon.

- Why are these fibres blended together?
- Find out the names given to these blends.
- Find examples of each one you name.

In this country, wool is popular for its warmth and texture. The **woolmark** symbol is used to show that a product is made of pure wool. (Pure wool has no more than five per cent of other fibres added.)

- Camel, angora, mohair and alpaca are animal fibres which are sometimes used instead of sheep's wool.

However, items made from pure wool are expensive and difficult to care for. For these reasons, wool is often blended with other fibres. The **woolblend** symbol is used to show this.

- Find out which fibres are blended together with wool.

Investigate

1 Find examples of fabrics that have been
   a) Woven
   b) Knitted
2 List the different properties of each type. (For example, you could compare a jumper or a cardigan with trousers or a skirt.)

The finishing touch

Fabrics can also have special finishes given to them. These add further properties such as flameproofing and waterproofing.

Brainstorm

1 Which other finishes do you know of?
2 Can you find or name some fabrics or items which have these finishes?

As you can see, we live in a world of fabrics. We now rely on them much more than ever before because they can be used in so many different ways. In fact, it could be said that it would be impossible to live without most of the fabrics around us. Don't you agree?

EXTENSION WORK *Investigate*

1 Pick a fabric.
2 What properties does it have?
3 Find out how it was made.
4 Find out why it has the properties that you have listed.
5 List the different ways in which this fabric could be used, as a result of the different properties that it has.

Investigate

1 Choose an item that has been made from fabric.
2 Trace the development of this item since it was first invented.
3 What changes have taken place in
   a) Design of the item?
   b) Fabrics used in the item?
4 Why have these changes taken place?

UNIT 8

Don't be a washout!

How do you feel about having new clothes? Do you feel happy? Do you feel like a 'new person'? Do you feel excited? Try to describe your feelings to a friend.

But what about this . . .

Have you ever found yourself in any of these situations?

Maybe you wouldn't wear clothes that have been ruined in this way! But there are very few people who haven't washed clothes at the wrong temperature, or dried them incorrectly, or scorched them with an iron at some time.

Have you got any stories to tell of clothes that are shrunken? Pink instead of white? Stretched out of shape beyond all recognition?!!!

● Share a few of your stories with other people in your class.

Some of the stories may seem very funny. It's all right if it only happens once in a while or if it happens to an old article of clothing.

● What if you are always ruining your clothes?
● What if you ruin something new or special?

This can be very expensive and very disappointing ... so what can you do?

Work out the code ...

All fabrics have a care label inside them.

This tells you how to wash, dry and iron the fabric.

It would be impossible to write out all the instructions in full sentences because they would take up too much room. So a special code is used.

The code has four main symbols:

1   tells you the washing instructions.

2   tells you the drying instructions.

3   tells you the ironing instructions.

4   (P)   is a dry-cleaning instruction.

- Where can you find full details of the care labelling code?
- Try to find a copy.

Investigate

1 Look through your clothes at home and household fabric items to find as many different care labels as you can.
2 Make a note of where you found each label and the fabric that each item was made from.
3 Find out what each label means.
4 Make a display of your findings in a table to show the others in your class.

Care label	Clothing/household item	Name of fabric used	What the label means

5 Which care labels are the most common?
6 Why do you think this is?

Testing, testing, testing . . .

If you don't believe how important it can be to read the care labels in things, have a go at these experiments.

Experiment 1 – Looking at wash temperatures

1 Collect five squares of dirty cotton fabric.
2 Collect five knitted wool squares.
3 Keep one square of each as a control.
4 Wash the cotton and wool squares in the following ways:
   a) A cold water wash
   b) A gentle hand-hot wash
   c) A medium temperature machine wash
   d) A long, hot wash in a washing machine
5 Leave each one to dry.
6 Compare each square to the control.

Questions

1 Which washing temperature is best for cotton?
2 Which washing temperature is best for wool?
3 Why did you have to leave them all to dry in the same way?
4 Why did you need a control?

Experiment 2 – Looking at drying clothes

1 Collect three pairs of thick (winter) tights (or machine knit three rectangles of wool).
2 Measure the length of each pair of tights or rectangle. Make a note of these measurements.
3 **a)** Wash one pair (or rectangle) and hang them up to drip dry.
   b) Wash one pair (or rectangle) and spin-dry them.
   c) Wash one pair (or rectangle) and pat them gently with a towel. Leave them to dry on a flat surface.
4 When all the items are dry, measure them again.
5 Compare these measurements to the first ones.
6 Which method of drying was best for keeping the shape of the tights? Why do you think this was?
7 Can you think of any other stretchy garments that might go out of shape if they are not dried correctly?

Experiment 3 – Looking at iron temperatures

Use an old iron for this!

1 Collect two crumpled or creased pieces of each of these fabrics
   a) Cotton
   b) Wool
   c) Nylon or terylene
2 Iron one piece of each with a 'cool' iron.
3 Iron the other pieces with a 'very hot' iron.

Questions

1 What happened to each piece of fabric at each temperature?
2 Which temperature is best for
   a) Cotton?
   b) Nylon?

'Persil' washes whiter . . . or does it?

There are lots of washing powders and liquids on sale today.

- Brainstorm the names of all the ones you can think of.
- Do you know the differences between them?

Washing powders aren't all exactly the same. In fact, they can be made up of quite complicated chemical mixtures. This means they will have different washing properties, and can do different jobs.

For example, some washing powders are good at removing grease. Some are good at working on certain stains (like blood, egg or gravy). Others are made for delicate fabrics or fabrics with special finishes. Some are even designed to work at lower water temperatures.

Investigate

1 Make a study of some popular washing powders.
2 Find out which ingredients are added to the various different washing powders.
3 Find out what these ingredients do.

Clothes will last longer and look nicer if they are well cared for. In this unit we have looked at the importance of washing, drying and ironing clothes correctly. There are other things to think about if you want your clothes to look nice.

Can you think of these?

Brainstorm

1 As a group make a list of all the things you need to do to keep your clothes in good condition.

EXTENSION WORK

Survey

1 Carry out a survey of several brands of washing powders of your choice.
2 Find out which ones give you the best value for money.
3 Make a display of your results and conclusions.

Investigate

1 Make a study of some television or magazine advertisements for washing powders.
2 How do the advertisements persuade people to buy the product?

Design

1 Devise an advertising campaign for a new washing powder.
2 As a class, display your ideas and decide upon the most persuasive advertisement.

UNIT 9

Textiles and the consumer

A consumer?

What's this got to do with textiles?

Anything and everything! For one thing, we are all consumers! If you go out and buy, hire or rent any kind of goods or services, then you are a consumer. So, whether you're buying food or clothes, bicycles or cars, you are a consumer.

As a consumer you have certain rights. For example,

- The goods you buy should be fit for the purpose. In other words they actually do what they should do!
- You are compensated for poor quality goods. You may be given your money back or given an exchange in return for what you bought.
- You are protected by Consumer Laws.

These laws have been set up to help you, as a consumer. If you buy something and it goes wrong, the laws are there to make sure you can get your money back or have the goods replaced.

BUT! In return, as a consumer you have certain responsibilities... These are that:

- You check goods before you buy them to see that they aren't faulty.
- You read any guarantees that are with the product.
- You know where to get help if things go wrong.

It's always a good idea to keep a receipt for the goods you buy. Then if things go wrong you can return the product and get a refund.

If you still aren't happy with what a shop offers when you complain then you can go to one of the consumer protection agencies. For example, the Trading Standards Office.

You can find out more about this from your local Citizens Advice Bureau.

Investigate

The **Sale of Goods Act** and the **Trade Descriptions Act** are two laws which protect you as a consumer.

1 Find out how these laws protect you. What do they say? What are your rights?
2 How do these two laws help you when you are buying textiles products? Try to think of some situations when the laws are broken. What could you do?

Investigate

1 Find out about the work done by the consumer agencies mentioned above.
2 Where can they be found?

Let's advertise it!

If you wanted to sell something what would you do? Firstly, you would want to let people know that you had something to sell.

To do this you would write an advertisement. Advertising is all around us. For example, we see it on television, in the street, at sporting events and in shops.

Observe

1 Look at these pictures which show some different places where you can find advertisements.

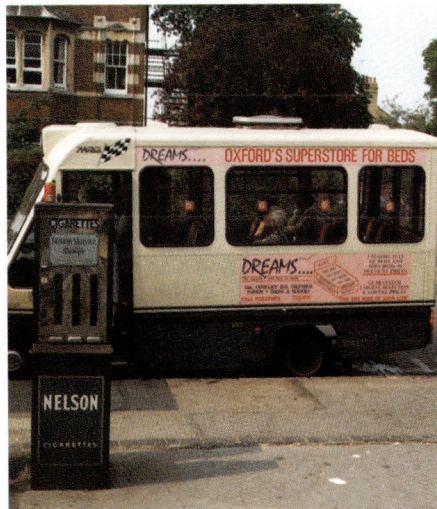

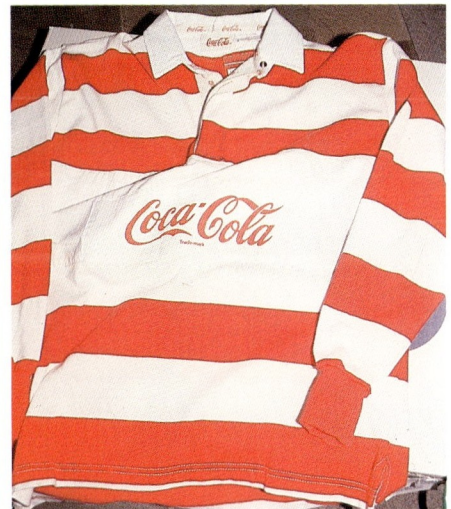

2 Can you add some ideas of your own to these?

Wherever an advertisement is found and whatever you are selling, the advertisement needs to do several things. It needs to

● Catch your eye
● Persuade you to buy
● Give some information about the product

Discuss

1 How do advertisements do each of these? Talk about your ideas with the rest of your class.

Investigate

1 Make a collection of some advertisements of your choice.
2 Try to decide how each advertisement
   a) Catches your eye
   b) Persuades people to buy
3 Try to decide who or what type of person the advertisements are aimed at.
4 What information does the advertisement give about the product?

It's got to have appeal . . .

Persuading people to buy a product is not always an easy task. Very often it is a case of finding out what appeals most to different people. The advertising industry spends a lot of time carrying out research to find out what makes people buy certain products.

These are some of the techniques that advertisers might use.

- **Snob appeal.** These advertisements suggest that the product is a real luxury to have.
- **Emotional appeal.** These advertisements suggest that if you buy the product you'll have a better lifestyle.
- **Sex appeal.** These advertisements suggest that if you use the product you'll attract the opposite sex.

1 In groups collect as many advertisements as you can for textile products.
2 Sort the advertisements into the different groups described above. For example, you might think a lot of them fit into the snob appeal group.

  • You may need to read the advertisement carefully to decide which group they fit into. You cannot always just go by the picture.

3 Not all the advertisements will fit into these groupings. Can you think of your own ways of grouping any you have left? For example, the advertisements may have the following images.

  • Fun loving   • Traditional
  • Youthful   • Comfort/security

4 Share your ideas with another group. Do you agree about the messages given by the advertisements?

Design

1 Choose one of the ways of grouping advertisements.
2 Design your own advertisement for a textile product which would fit in with that group.

Labels – to protect you . . .

Labels play an important role in consumer protection.

The information given on them has to be set out clearly. It also has to be correct. In other words, a jumper described as being 'pure wool' on the label has to be made of 'pure wool'. It also has to have clear washing instructions as we discussed in Unit 8.

Investigate

1 Make a collection of labels from textile products.
2 What sort of information can you find on the labels? Make a list of your findings.

Special treatment?

How to care for it?

```
46% COTTON
46% POLYESTER
8% ELASTANE
ONE SIZE
MADE IN U.K.
```

Size of garment?

Fibre content?

```
[wash symbols]
HAND WASH
DO NOT BLEACH
WARM IRON
TUMBLE DRY
DRY CLEANABLE
WASH SEPARATELY
```

Manufacturer's name?

Where it's been made

Of course some of the information also helps the manufacturers.

● A label can be an advertisement ...

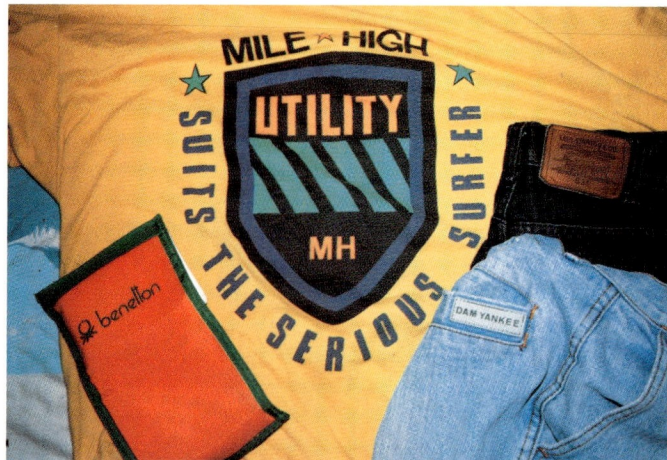

● It can also protect the manufacturer. You cannot have your money back on a pair of jeans that have shrunk if the label tells you they may shrink when you wash them.
Nor can you have your money back on a damaged article if you tumble dry it when the label says not to.

As you can see it's certainly worth getting to know and understand the labels on the textile products you buy!

Unit 8 looks at this in more detail.

Investigate

1 What information would you expect to see on labels for each of these items:
   a) A pure wool jumper
   b) A cotton shirt
   c) A waterproof jacket
   d) A 100% wool coat with a 100% triacetate lining

EXTENSION WORK

Discuss

You buy a pair of trousers. They shrink badly even though you followed the instructions on the care label. You take the trousers back to the shop. The shop refuses to refund or exchange the trousers.

1 What should you do?
2 Try to act out a scene to show your solution to this problem.

Design

1 Design your own label or logo for one of the following.
   a) A new range of sportswear
   b) A new design of hard-wearing jeans
   c) A new range of 'fashion' clothes

Remember to think about the kind of image you want the clothing to have!

UNIT 10
High technology!

Have you ever noticed just how much things change over time?

Look at the changes that have taken place in the design of the bicycle since the penny-farthing at the beginning of this century.

- Why have these changes taken place?
- What do you think will happen over the next twenty years?

There are several reasons why such changes take place. One reason is that the original design of a piece of equipment needs improving. This may make the equipment do its job better. It may make it perform more efficiently.

So, change takes place to improve performance.

Have you ever bought something and after a while found yourself thinking how it could be improved?

- What did you buy?
- How could it have been improved?

Very often, it's not until we start using something that we can see where improvement is needed. This is how we make progress!

It is one thing to say HOW something needs to be improved. It is quite another to be ABLE to make those improvements.

Advances in technology have allowed us to make most of the improvements that we feel are needed.

A BMX bicycle is much more robust than a penny-farthing. It can stand up to much greater use ... and misuse! Imagine doing 'wheelies' on a penny-farthing!!

Similarly, a lot of the clothes you are wearing, or the equipment you use at home have been improved over the years. Fabrics used for clothing can be made to last longer or to hold their shape better. Technological advances, for example, have made towels more absorbent and more comfortable to use.

All the time, progress is being made. Progress which relies on technology and the ability to use that technology.

Investigate

1 Choose any item in the house (or outside it) that is of interest to you.
2 Trace the development of that item since it was invented.
3 Present your findings to the rest of your class.

Design for living . . .

Technological advances are one reason for change. There are others. We've already said that things are changed because they need to be improved. But this doesn't really explain all the different styles and colours of things that are used.

A BMX bicycle may be a better performer than a penny-farthing, but why are there so many different colours and design logos available? Does the colour and design logo make any difference to the performance?

No, of course not!!

Colours, patterns and styles are things that change with time, too. But they are not essential changes! A black BMX is just as good at doing the job as a purple one! These changes are simply to do with

fashion and image. They are brought about by the designers and image-setters in the design world.

You're only human . . .

It's only human to want to improve what you've got. When you first learned to ride a bicycle, all that mattered was that you had a bicycle to ride. It didn't really matter what it looked like, or what it could do, as long as it had two wheels and you could ride it!

Once you have learned to ride, you start to want more than just a basic bicycle. You want gears for changing speed, you want handlebars that are lower – or higher! You want the latest design and colour. In other words, 'extra' features become important. A bicycle with all the extras gives you a feeling of confidence. People admire your bicycle – it gives you some kind of status.

Of course, not everybody feels like this, but many people do.

- How many of you would be happy to ride around on a penny-farthing?
- How many of you would feel silly?

Bicycles are just one example of how we choose things because they are stylish and in fashion, as well as because they do a job.

A lot of equipment that is bought for your home is chosen in the same way.

When you first set up home you may be happy to fill it with things that simply 'do the job'. Styles and fashion may not bother you. Then after a while you start to want certain colours and designs. These aren't essential, but they are part of your wanting to be up-to-date and stylish.

Investigate

1 Pick a basic household item (for example, bedding, towels, kitchen equipment, radios or televisions).
2 Find out what styles and colours are in fashion at the moment.
3 What styles and colours were fashionable five years ago? Ten years ago? (Ask your parents or friends.)
4 How have things changed?
5 What do you think will be the fashion in ten years time?

Design

1 Design a 'new', updated version of the item you studied in the last investigation.
2 Choose a new style and colour range for the item.
3 Present your ideas and sketches to the rest of your class.

Design

1 Design an advertising campaign for the new style and range of equipment you have developed.

2 How would you advertise your range? What image would it have?
3 Where would you advertise your range? On television? In magazines?
4 Present your ideas to the rest of your class.

EXTENSION WORK   *Investigate*

Why do people buy what they do?

1 Talk to a friend or a member of your family who has bought something new recently.
2 Ask them why they bought the item or equipment.

For example, a new car may have been bought for its colour, its comfort, better mileage, more features
or
because it looked good in the advertisements!

See what you can find out!

Investigate

1 Find out how your school uniform (if your wear one) has been updated over the last ten years.
2 How do people update the uniform as individuals? Try to get hold of photographs of your parents' or grandparents' school uniform or sportswear.
3 How has it been updated today?

Investigate

1 Investigate the range of bedding and matching accessories that you can buy today.
2 Collect samples or photos to illustrate what you have found.

3 Compare your findings to the styles of the 1950s or 1960s.

- What changes have taken place?
- How different are the styles or colours used?

Design

You have been given some money to decorate your bedroom.

1 Design your own co-ordinated bedding and accessory range for your room.
2 Explain your choice of design.

UNIT 11
Clothing and culture

The style of dress or clothing that people wear is an important part of their culture. A person's culture is formed by the way she or he has lived since birth.

Throughout the world there are many different cultures. As a result, there are also many different styles of dress.

Nowadays people in many countries often choose 'western' dress for everyday wear. They may keep their traditional clothing for special occasions. Of course, this has not always been the case. Advances in technology have led to people changing their styles of clothing. Television has meant that people can see what kind of clothes are worn in different countries. Better transport systems have meant that people can buy clothes from different countries without having to pay too much for them.

- Try to think of some special occasions when you might wear traditional styles of dress.
- Share your ideas with a friend.

In this unit you will look at the styles of dress and cultures of some different countries around the world.

China and Japan

Most people think of the **kimono** when they are asked about traditional Japanese clothing. The kimono is made from strips of fabric sewn together and shaped at the collar, lapels and sleeves. It was the Chinese who developed the kimono. The Japanese people then began to use it but mainly as an undergarment. In the humid climate of Japan, the kimono was very comfortable as it was loose fitting and usually made of 'cool' fabrics like cotton or silk.

On the other hand, in north-east China, the cold winters meant that people needed to wear layers of clothing. Both men and women wore trousers for warmth. Sometimes they would pad their clothes with wool or silk for extra protection against the cold.

Symbolic meanings . . .

Chinese clothing often had symbols on it. These symbols might be dragons, tigers, unicorns or phoenix. They would each have a special meaning.

For example,

- The dragon represented imperial power
- The phoenix represented peace and good fortune
- The unicorn meant grandeur
- The tiger meant courage

Design

1 Design some symbols that you might like to wear.
2 Explain your designs to the rest of the class.

Colour was also important in Chinese clothing. The five elements, water, metal, earth, fire and wood, were represented by the colours black, white, yellow, red and green. Yellow was the main colour. It stood for the Earth and the centre of the universe. The Emperor and his family often wore this colour.

The Japanese also like to decorate their clothing. This was often done to show which particular class or family they were from. Some women would decorate their kimonos with gold and silver embroidery. This was a sign that they were wealthy.

1 Carry out a study of how Chinese or Japanese fashions have changed over the years. Present your findings to the rest of your class.

India

In India, the traditional dress for women is called a **sari**. For most Indian men it is the **dhoti.**

Before man-made fibres were introduced, the clothing was made from cotton. Cotton grows well in warm, moist climates such as India.

Peru

In Peru traditional clothing is still worn by many tribes – people who live in the Andes mountains. Many of these people are farmers and crafts people. Their main form of clothing is the **poncho.**

The poncho is a large square of fabric with a hole made in the centre to put your head through. It is usually made from wool.

Believe it or not, the poncho was a fashion item in this country in the 1970s! Many people knitted or crocheted bright squares of wool and made them into ponchos.

The wool which is used comes from the goats or sheep kept by the tribal people. Sometimes llama or alpaca wool is used. These wools produce a longer thicker fibre and make a coarser fibre for spinning for two main reasons. Firstly, it has a natural **crimp** (or waviness) which makes spinning easier. Secondly, it is oily. This is because of the lanolin – the natural grease in wool.

EXTENSION WORK   *Investigate*

1 Find out about the traditional clothing worn by other cultures not covered in this unit.

- Find out which fabrics are used and why.
- Show how fashions have changed over the years for the culture you are studying.

Index